THE
SIMPLE GUIDE
TO
MAASTRICHT

PETER LUFF
DIRECTOR OF THE EUROPEAN MOVEMENT

About the Author

Peter Luff has been the Director of the European Movement since 1987. Born in Brussels and educated in the UK, he took a degree in Politics and International Relations at the University College of Wales, Swansea.

After working with the Voluntary Committee for Overseas Aid and Development and the UK Immigrants Advisory Service, he travelled around the world and then took the post of Assistant Director of Amnesty International (UK). He spent a short time at the BBC before becoming the Funding and Marketing Director of the Social Democratic Party between 1982 -87.

Peter Luff lectures and broadcasts regularly on European Affairs and is a Fellow of the Royal Society of Arts and Manufactures and the Royal Geographical Society.

Acknowledgements

Considerable help and encouragement was received in the preparation of this booklet from John Pinder, Ernest Wistrich, Stephen Woodard, Sir Anthony Meyer, Carolyn Luff, John Parry and Andrew Duff. The author also wishes to thank Bernadine Adkins for her invaluable legal advice and the London Offices of the Commission and the European Parliament from whose explanations of the Maastricht Treaty, he has borrowed freely and shamelessly.

Copyright European Movement 1992

European Movement
Published 1992

ISBN 1 873113 06 4

INDEX

Foreword
Introduction. 1

PART ONE
Chapter
1   Why is the Maastricht Treaty Necessary? 6
2   A Summary of the Treaty 8

PART TWO
Chapter
3   Beginning at the Beginning 13
4   Turning the EEC into the European Community 15
5   The Principles of Economic and Monetary Union 18
6   Subsidiarity 22
7   Citizenship of the Union 23
8   Reforming the Institutions 25
9   General Provisions applying to the EC 28
10 A Common Foreign and Security Policy...........................34
11 Justice & Home Affairs 37
12 The Social Dimension 39
13 Budgetary Control 40

PART THREE
Chapter
14 Europe, Past, Present and Future. 42
15 The Congress of Europe 43
16 The Treaty of Rome...45
17 The Single European Act..49
18 Enlargement of the Community 52
19 The Institutions of the European Community 53

PART FOUR
Chapter
20 10 Myths About the Maastricht Treaty 56

Foreword

By Rt Hon. Sir Michael Palliser, GCMG
Chairman of the European Movement Advisory Council

What were, and are, the basic tenets of post-war European unity, which we will only forget at our peril?

They were, in the first instance, to contain and restrain the aggressive nationalisms that had resulted in so many wars down the centuries in Europe, especially between France and Germany; to find a framework within which to contain Germany itself; to build, with American support, a strong defence against Communism; to create a real economic and financial common market that would strengthen European prosperity in the member countries and the competitive strength of Europe in world markets; and, finally, to form a political and economic community that would both regulate and govern the common market and give the Community an effective voice in world affairs.

These basics all still obtain. True, we no longer have to face the threat of Soviet Communism: but it has been replaced by the need to contain a new set of nationalisms within what used to be the Soviet Union and to help stabilise its most unstable former empire. What was fundamental in the fifties is still fundamental today. The safety, the prosperity and the influence of our free society in the world, and the European democracy on which it is based, still require the development of a European Community that is strong and self-confident enough to avoid us moving back into the self-destructive world of nation states that we have slowly been leaving behind us, with inestimable benefit to us all.

So I say with all the conviction at my command that all of us in Europe - especially in the confused aftermath of the Danish and French referenda - have to keep a firm grasp on the fundamental needs and aspirations of our society, which the Community enshrines, and very firmly to reject the arguments of those who are exploiting the situation for destructive purposes.

There are siren voices which tell us that Europe can and should rely in the future on a return to a system of loose alliances between nation states, if necessary against Germany. Back to the 19th century - and to hell, literally, with the future.

This is incredibly perverse. Its main effect would be to ensure that Germany really did become the dominant power in Europe, though not at all necessarily a malevolent one. And a score of other problems would remain unsolved. The truth is that the need to reaffirm the aims and ideals of European Union, whatever the form it may acquire, has become all the greater with Germany united, new nationalisms emerging on both sides of what we used to call the Iron Curtain, American influence wavering and uncertain and the global economy becoming ever more competitive.

What we need now is a fresh campaign throughout the European Community and beyond in Europe to remind all the people not only that the Maastricht Treaty would in fact strengthen democratic control in the Community and especially in Brussels: but also that the fundamental historical reasons for pursuing European Union are just as valid and just as powerful today as they ever have been.

I warmly welcome the publication of this timely guide to the Maastricht Treaty and hope it is widely read.

(Sir Michael Palliser was formerly Head of the UK Delegation to the European Communities in Brussels 1971, Ambassador and Permanent Representative to the European Communities 1973-75, Permanent Under-Secretary of State at the Foreign and Commonwealth Office, and Head of the Diplomatic Service 1975-82. He is presently Chairman of Samuel Montagu Co Ltd.)

Introduction

★ ★ ★ ★ ★ ★ ★ ★ ★ ★ ★ ★ ★

To be honest, the Maastricht Treaty is not simple. It is a legal document that will be binding on the signatories and it certainly does not make for easy reading.

Not only does it use words such as "Economic and Monetary Union", "subsidiarity" and "Political Union", which are rarely explained or defined in the press and other media, but it also establishes a whole new idea, that of "European Union", at a time when most people are still struggling to work out how, when and why the "Common Market" turned into the European Community.

It is further complicated by the fact that it looks at times like a sack into which a number of useful but very different objects have been crammed. Large and extremely complicated issues like Economic and Monetary Union (EMU) and foreign and security cooperation stick out at the sides, while equally important but more straightforward issues such as the principle of European citizenship and new powers for the European Parliament tend to look a little lost in the jumble in the middle.

Nevertheless, once the legal jargon has been removed, the Maastricht Treaty contains nothing that cannot be understood by anyone who understands something of the history and structure of the European Community and is prepared to spend a short time reading. It is a logical, if a little untidy, progression towards the goal of European Unity that has been the aim of the European Community since it began forty years ago.

At this point, there will be some readers who will say "Stop! We don't have an understanding of the history of the Community. That is part of the problem. Although we know we are in it, no-one has bothered to explain clearly why it was formed, what is its purpose and how it actually works."

With this major problem in mind, the second half of this booklet provides a brief history of the European Community and a guide to the institutions and how they work. Hopefully, it will help to place the Treaty into a context and show that it is not the brainchild of zealous Euro-fanatics but a response both to changing economic conditions and to the increasing need to make the institutions of the Community more democratic and accountable.

There will also be some people who do not consider a seventy page booklet should call itself "simple". There is, of course, a great difference between "simple" and "brief", but for those who just want a short outline of what is in the Treaty, it can be found in Chapter 2.

Selling the Treaty

With hindsight, a smart marketing executive would have suggested many ways to make the Treaty more attractive and comprehensible. At the same time, he or she might have spent some time before it was put before the people of Europe, explaining why it was necessary and what needs it was designed to fill.

Unfortunately, this did not happen and it is now quite obvious that many people throughout Europe are not only puzzled about what the Treaty actually says but do not fully understand why it is necessary and what it may mean for their lives and jobs.

As we have seen in Denmark and in France, this has led to considerable disquiet about its ratification by the member states.

If it were merely a question of creating problems for the institutions of the Community or the governments of the member states which have invested so much time in its negotiation, one might be tempted to send them back to the drawing board to begin again.

But the issue is not as simple as that. It is not just a matter of discomfort for the politicians and the bureaucrats; it is of vital importance for each and every person throughout the whole Community that the Treaty is ratified and comes into force as swiftly as possible.

Not only could its rejection plunge the Community into uncertainty and confusion at a time when both internal and external economic and political problems require unity and a renewed sense of purpose, but it would also mean that crucial reforms designed to make the existing structures more open and accountable would be lost.

Many people, while being sympathetic to the principles of European integration, are extremely irritated by the feeling that the Community is increasingly intruding into too many aspects of what they believe should be outside its competence. Although many of these petty aggravations in fact originate from the member states, who take convenient refuge in blaming the Community, the feelings of anger and hostility they cause are very real. Contained within the Maastricht Treaty are the first steps towards defining more clearly at which level decisions should be taken: it would be ironical in the extreme if such reforms were lost because they were not properly understood.

The Treaty is not a perfect document; something that represents a hard fought compromise between the national interests of twelve countries rarely is. Nevertheless, its critics have singularly failed to offer an alternative. It is very simple to say "Go back to the drawing board", but no-one can show how this process would come up with anything better; indeed, it is almost certain that the disillusion that would accompany a failure to ratify the

Treaty would either bring confusion or a far more unsatisfactory document.

But this booklet is not designed to serve as propaganda. It aims to set out in clear language the main points of the Treaty, to place it in the context of the origins and development of the European Community and to explain the work of the Community's main institutions.

In no way does it pretend to provide a comprehensive analysis of each and every clause of the Treaty. Sometimes, clauses which are clear and readable may be quoted in full; usually, a summary is given of the proposals setting out the main points. Clearly, this means that some details, which may be considered of great importance by some specialists, may be omitted. The alternative would be to reprint and analyse the Treaty clause by clause and, while such documents are available to the British public,* this booklet is intended to serve a different purpose.

As far as possible, it will avoid the use of acronyms except when it becomes too tedious to write the names in full each time, for example EC rather than European Community. For reference purposes, the letters and numbers heading the main articles and clauses have occasionally been listed but only where further reference was thought useful. To the lay reader they may seem an untidy jumble of Arabic and Roman numerals and large and small letters. This is because the Treaty is both an amendment to previous treaties and also sets out new ideas of its own.

But, although every effort has been taken to make sure that the information provided is accurate and balanced, it would be foolish to pretend that the authors are neutral in the debate that is taking place about the future of Europe.

Ever since it was founded by Sir Winston Churchill and other great post-war leaders, the European Movement has argued that

---

*For example: The New Treaty on European Union, Belmont European Policy Centre, 42, Boulevard Charlemagne, Brussels, Belgium. tel: 010 322 321 0340 2 volumes.

the only way to preserve peace and promote prosperity in Europe is to move towards "an ever closer union of peoples". This has been our creed but we fully understand that it will not happen unless the peoples of Europe themselves understand the goal and are willing to participate in its realisation.

PART ONE

Chapter 1

Why is the Maastricht Treaty Necessary?
★ ★ ★ ★ ★ ★ ★ ★ ★ ★ ★ ★ ★

There was a considerable sense of relief on the part of the leaders of the 12 member states of the European Community, and the President of the Commission, when, in the early hours of the morning of December 11 1991, in the historic Dutch town of Maastricht, they agreed the text of a Treaty on European Union , 17 associated protocols (additional agreements between some but not all the signatories), and 33 Declarations, which do not have legal force but outline the ways in which the provisions of the Treaty should be interpreted or implemented.

It was the culmination of long and arduous negotiations that had followed the reports of two inter-governmental conferences (IGCs) between the 12 member states - one on Economic & Monetary Union and the other on Political Union - which had been created to look at ways the Community should meet the new circumstances created by the imminent completion of the single market and the revolutionary changes taking place in central and eastern Europe.

As the key objectives of the single market - the free movement of goods, people, capital and services - approached completion, new opportunities and problems were being created that needed urgent attention.

For example, the free movement of capital could lead both to dangerous runs on the weaker currencies - as has been recently and dramatically illustrated - and to the possibility that one currency could become overwhelmingly dominant, with all the political imbalance that would imply.

Business within the single market was also pressing for an end to fluctuating and uncertain exchange rates which imposed increasing problems for the movement of goods and services within the Community. Individual travellers, for business or pleasure, find it increasingly irksome to pay commission to the banks and lose the difference between buying and selling rates. It was agreed that the solution to these problems was to move towards Economic and Monetary Union (EMU), with a single currency the ECU (European Currency Unit) that could be used freely throughout the Community.

At the same time, it was widely recognised that any move towards EMU that would increase the powers of the Community, should be balanced by a strengthening of the democratic accountability of the Community, most especially the power of the European Parliament, and by ensuring that all decisions should be taken as closely as possible to the citizens of Europe.

Europe's failure to react swiftly and decisively to crises on its doorstep, notably the Gulf War and the conflict in what had been previously Yugoslavia, illustrated the urgent need for mechanisms that would allow for far greater foreign and security policy cooperation.

Added to that, the desire to allow Europe's citizens to share common political and social rights, the need for a number of small but significant changes to Community procedures, and the wish of some members states to see the new Union develop some of its activities through inter-governmental rather than integrated Community institutions, and the Maastricht Treaty began to assume its present complex form which has done so much to confuse people throughout Europe.

Although the agreement was signed in Maastricht, however, it cannot come into force until the text has been ratified by all twelve members states. In some cases, for example Denmark and Ireland, this process could only be completed after a popular referendum. In France, a referendum, though not constitutionally necessary, was called by the French President.

It is worth emphasising again that the Maastricht Treaty, like the Single European Act, amends the Treaty of Rome which was signed by the original 6 members of the EC in 1957 and to which the United Kingdom acceded in 1973. If the Maastricht Treaty is ratified by all 12 it will be incorporated into one unified text.

Chapter 2

A Summary of the Treaty
★ ★ ★ ★ ★ ★ ★ ★ ★ ★ ★ ★

There are *five* important ideas in the Maastricht Treaty that make it different in kind from the previous treaties.

★
★ **Five important**
★ **ideas in the**
★ **Maastricht**
★ **Treaty make it**
★ **different in**
★ **kind from the**
★ **previous**
★ **treaties.**
★

Firstly, it creates *"The European Union"* which amends the underlying structure of the way in which the twelve member states deal with each other.

What is the "European Union" and how does it differ from the European Community?

Very simply, it is a term given to the next stage in the process of integration between the 12 member states of the Community which, while developing and deepening the work of the Community as a whole, creates two more pillars of activity which will be largely conducted on an inter-governmental basis.

Although the member states wanted to go further towards greater integration, some of them did not want to give much more power to the Community's institutions as a whole.

Whereas previously, most decisions were made through the institutions of the European Community (EC), the new European Union created by the Maastricht Treaty establishes a three pillared structure, of which the European Community is just one, albeit the most important, pillar.

The *three* pillars of the European Union will look like this:

1. **The European Community** with, as before:

★ The COUNCIL of Ministers (relevant ministers from each country meeting on the issues which concern them i.e. trade, education, agriculture, environment etc., with twice a year, a meeting of the 12 nations' leaders called the European Council. It takes the final decisions on all EC legislation).

★ The EUROPEAN PARLIAMENT (518 members directly elected every five years. It can advise and amend EC laws and the EC budget).

★ The COMMISSION (17 Commissioners heading up 13,000 European civil servants. It proposes EC laws and supervises their implementation).

★ The COURT OF JUSTICE (Judges appointed from the member states. They rule on the interpretation and validity of EC laws and may fine countries which fail to comply with judgements of the Court). (Further details on the EC's institutions can be found in Chapter 19.)

2. **Common Foreign and Security Policy.**
To be agreed largely on an inter-governmental basis with some input from the other EC institutions.

3. Home Affairs and Justice Policy.

Again, to be largely agreed on an inter-governmental basis.

★ **The concept of**
★ **"subsidiarity"**
★ **ensures that**
★ **only those**
★ **decisions which**
★ **are strictly**
★ **necessary**
★ **should be taken**
★ **by Brussels**

Secondly, the Treaty establishes a principle in the European Union which re-enforces the concept of *"subsidiarity"*, whereby decisions should be taken at the lowest level compatible with efficiency and democracy or, putting it another way round, only those decisions which are strictly necessary should be taken by the centre, i.e. the institutions in Brussels rather than the relevant institutions in the member states. In reality, it is used in the Treaty to suggest which legislation should be adopted by the Community as a whole and which by the governments of the member states, and who should be responsible for its enforcement.

The principle of subsidiarity is designed to prevent a widespread, though not always accurate feeling, that citizens in the member states are having decisions made for them in Brussels that they would prefer to have taken either by their national, regional or local governments.

Thirdly, responding to a growing feeling in many member states, that the regions of Europe should have a greater say in the Community's future, a new *Committee of the Regions* is to be set up with, at this stage, responsibility to offer its advice and suggestions.

Fourthly, it sets out *a procedure and a timetable for creating Economic and Monetary Union (EMU)*. This is a process under which the existing currencies of the twelve member states will be replaced by a single currency controlled by a European Central Bank. The timetable suggested makes it possible for a single currency to be introduced in some member states as early as 1997, though more likely 1999. Only those countries whose economies have converged in accordance with criteria laid down will be able to adopt a single currency. The European Central Bank is to be an independent institution, free of political control, though answerable for its management to the Union's other institutions. Because the British Government was unwilling to commit itself, at this stage, to the principle of adopting a single currency it was allowed an opt-out clause in the Treaty. We will only join if Parliament agrees at some time in the future.

Fifthly, the Treaty establishes a new idea: that of *European citizenship*, which gives new, albeit limited, shared rights to all those who are presently citizens of the member states. Among these are the right for those living in member states other than their own, to stand, and to vote, in local and European elections, the right to be represented by Consuls of other member states if travelling in third countries (countries not in the Community), and the right to complain to a European Ombudsman about EC maladministration.

Further to these five new ideas, the Treaty also sets out to reform or enhance other Community structures and activities but these, while important, are not new in kind.

New and extended powers are given, under the Treaty, to the European Parliament. Although these do not go as far towards remedying what is called the "democratic deficit" - the lack of democracy in the Community's institutions - as many reformers might like, the Parliament will get greater powers to amend European legislation and, in some cases, to veto it.

★ ★ **The Maastricht** ★ **Treaty gives** ★ **new and** ★ **extended** ★ **powers to the** ★ **European** ★ **Parliament** ★

The drafters of the Treaty also sought to increase the Community's powers to enforce certain social rights and obligations but, because of the British government's refusal to accept this part of the Treaty, it was put into a separate protocol signed by the other eleven member states.

Various steps were agreed to tighten up the Community's finances:

★ when proposing new measures, the Commission must give assurances that they can be financed within the limits of European Community financial resources;

★ the status of the European Court of Auditors, who check that everything is in correct financial order, is enhanced as it becomes a full EC institution;

★ the European Parliament will be able to ask the Commission to give evidence regarding spending and financial control and the Commission will act on the decisions and observations of the Parliament;

★ Governments will be made to deal with fraud affecting the Community's financial interests in the same way that they deal with national fraud.

★ Finally, The Court of Justice is given greater powers to ensure that all member states meet their obligations to enforce Community legislation. Those who do not can be fined by the Court.

That was a summary. For those who wish to see the detail of the text, the following chapters set out and explain in greater detail the content of the Treaty.

PART TWO

Chapter 3

Beginning at the Beginning.
★ ★ ★ ★ ★ ★ ★ ★ ★ ★ ★ ★

Like most treaties, the Maastricht Treaty begins with a summary of its main objectives, most of which are straightforward and worth quoting in full. The first, in Article A, is that the 12 member states wish to establish a European Union.

As was explained previously, this new animal - the European Union - incorporates the European Community as one of its three pillars, but has wider objectives than those of the Community.

Article A continues:

> "This Treaty marks a new stage in the process of creating an ever closer Union among the peoples of Europe, where decisions are taken as closely as possible to the citizens".

Article B sets the Union the following objectives:

> "to promote economic and social progress which is balanced and sustainable, in particular through the creation of an area without internal frontiers, through the strengthening of economic and social cohesion and the establishment of economic and monetary union ultimately including a single currency in accordance with the provisions of the current Treaty."

NOTE: the "area without internal frontiers" refers to the completion of the single market; "economic and social cohesion" refers primarily to the process by which the richer countries and regions help the poorer ones to develop; and the "current Treaty" refers to the Treaty of Rome as amended by the Single European Act.

> *"to assert its (the European Union's) identity on the international scene, in particular through the implementation of a foreign and security policy, which shall include the eventual framing of a common defence policy."*

> *"to strengthen the protection of the rights and interests of the nationals of its member states through the introduction of a citizenship of the Union."*

> *" to develop close cooperation on justice and home affairs."*

Article F makes three important commitments:

> *"The Union shall respect the national identity of its member states, whose systems of government are founded on the principles of democracy."*

> *"The Union shall respect fundamental human rights as guaranteed by the European Convention for the Protection of Human Rights and Fundamental Freedoms as they result from the constitutional traditions common to the member states and as general principles of Community law."*

> *"The Union shall provide itself with the resources necessary to attain its objectives and carry through its policies."*

Having set out its objectives, the Treaty then sets out how it will achieve them.

Chapter 4

Turning the EEC
into the European Community *
★ ★ ★ ★ ★ ★ ★ ★ ★ ★ ★ ★ ★

Although the new European Union incorporates the European Community (EC), for many people the EC itself is an enigma as they always thought it was called the European Economic Community (EEC).

In fact, as the European Economic Community has had to deal with an increasing number of political, environmental and social issues, it became more logical to drop the qualifying word "economic". The Treaty of Maastricht, like the Single European Act, formalises this process by amending the Treaty of Rome and the Single European Act so that EEC can be changed to EC. It also reaffirms its key objectives, some of which are contained in the previous treaties and some of which are new and are referred to as "the Treaty".

As these set out very clearly the central underlying reasons for the European Community, they are worth listing in full:

Article 1 of the Treaty states that the 12 member states are establishing a European Community. (i.e. instead of the European Economic Community).

Article 2 lists the Community's main tasks:

★   a common market;

★   economic and monetary union;

---

* Just to complicate matters, there are in fact 3 communities: the Coal and Steel Community, EURATOM, and the Economic Community but for the sake of simplicity they are usually referred to as if they were one: the European Community.

★ sustainable and non-inflationary growth;

★ economic convergence;

★ respect for the environment;

★ a high level of employment and social protection;

★ raising living standards in member states;

★ economic and social cohesion;

★ creating solidarity between member states;

In addition to these broad and fundamental objectives, the Treaty also lists the following aims:

★ eliminating all customs duties and restrictions on importing and exporting goods within the Community;

★ introducing measures for a common immigration and visa policy into the Community;

★ providing for a common commercial policy;

★ removing any remaining obstacles to the free movement of people, goods, services and capital within the Community;

★ measures concerning the entry and movement of people in the internal market;

★ common policies in agriculture and fisheries;

★ a common policy in transport;

★ ensuring that competition is not distorted in the internal market;

★ approximising the laws of member states to the extent required for the functioning of a common market;

★ developing a common policy in the social sphere comprising a European Social Fund;

★ promoting research and technological development;

★ encouraging the establishment and development of trans-European networks;

★ contributing to the attainment of a high level of health protection;

★ contributing to high quality education and training and to the flowering of the cultures of member states;

★ co-ordinating policy in the sphere of overseas development cooperation;

★ contributing to the strengthening of consumer protection; and

★ measures in the spheres of energy, civil protection and tourism.

Essentially these principles summarise the whole idea of the European Community and all other legislation derives from them.

But remember that the Community is only one of the three pillars of European Union as set out in the Maastricht Treaty. The other two are foreign and security policy cooperation and justice and home affairs.

Chapter 5

The Principles of
Economic and Monetary Union
★ ★ ★ ★ ★ ★ ★ ★ ★ ★ ★ ★

The aim of Economic and Monetary Union is to create a single currency for the European Community that can be used in shops and banks as well as in the money markets and to settle accounts between countries. Despite the use of the world "union" in its title, Economic and Monetary Union comes under the auspices of the European Community and is not a separate pillar. It aims to benefit citizens both in business and in their daily lives by removing the uncertainty of exchange rate fluctuations, lowering inflation and interest rates, removing the need and, therefore the cost, of changing money between member states, and by providing stable prices and a powerful world currency in competition with the US dollar and the Japanese yen.

★ **EMU aims to**
★ **reduce**
★ **exchange rate**
★ **fluctuations,**
★ **lower inflation**
★ **and interest**
★ **rates and**
★ **provide**
★ **stable prices**

A common currency would also remove the possibility of speculation against member states' individual currencies and would help end the boom/bust cycle of economic activity that has hurt sustained economic growth. It would also ensure that monetary policy in Europe is controlled by all member states together rather than dominated by any single large national economy.

Article 3A obliges the member states to adopt an economic policy based on close co-ordination of their economic policies in accordance with the principle of an open market economy and free competition in order to achieve the economic convergence necessary for monetary union.

The article continues by committing the member states to an irrevocable fixing of exchange rates which will lead to the introduction of a single currency (the ECU), and the definition and conduct of a single monetary policy and exchange rate policy.

The primary objectives of these policies will be to maintain price stability and to support the general economic objectives of the Community.

Finally, article 3A sets out guidelines as to the kind of principles which must underlie these economic policies, which include: stable prices, sound public finances and monetary conditions and a sustainable balance of payments.

Article 4A calls for the establishment of a European System of Central banks (ESCB) whose powers are defined later in the Treaty.

The details of Economic and Monetary Union are spelt out in great detail in articles 102 through to 109. Not unexpectedly, they are complex and numerous and it would take too much space to go into all their provisions. Instead, this chapter will provide a summary outlining the key ideas and dates in the proposed timetable for the achievement of Economic and Monetary Union.

The details and the timetable of EMU

Progress towards Economic and Monetary Union is in three stages:-

Stage 1 began on July 1 1990 with action being taken to improve co-operation and co-ordination between members states in the economic and monetary fields, to strengthen the European Monetary System and the role of the ECU and to extend the work of the Committee of the Governors of the member states' central banks. (In the UK, this is the Bank of England).

Stage 1 was launched under existing European Community powers but stages 2 and 3 depend upon the Maastricht Treaty amending the Treaty of Rome because they involve creating new institutions.

The Treaty outlines the following timetable:

Stage 2 is planned to begin on January 1 1994 with the establishment of a European Monetary Institute (EMI) charged with the task of promoting the co-ordination of member states' economic policies to bring about EMU. By then, each member state should have adopted programmes to achieve greater convergence. The Commission and the EMI will report on progress of member states towards convergence. Their findings will then go to the European Council which will decide whether a majority of member states have met the four convergence criteria, which are:

★ price stability: a rate of inflation no more than 1.5% above the average of the three best performing member states;

★ interest rates should not be more than 2 percentage points above the average of these three best performing states over the previous 12 months;

★ there should be no excessive government deficit i.e. not above 3% of GDP; public debt should not exceed 60% of GDP;

★ exchange rate fluctuations in the European Monetary System (EMS) should not exceed their normal margins for at least two years;

Stage 3 may begin on December 31 1996 if the European Council takes a qualified majority decision that enough member states have met the criteria to form a "critical mass" to move forward to monetary union. This would mean that 7 out of the 12 member states, or 6 out of 11, if Britain was not taking part, meet the convergence criteria. The date for completion would then be fixed.

If it had not already happened by then, the creation of a European Central Bank (ECB) and a European System of Central Banks would begin in 1998. This would also be the date by which national central banks would become independent if the ECB and ESCB were not already in place.

★ **The ECU will be**
★ **a currency** ●
★ **usable in shops**
★ **and banks in all**
★ **those countries**
★ **that have**
★ **moved to full**
★ **monetary union**
★

If by the end of 1997, the date for the beginning of stage 3 had not already been set, it would begin irrevocably on January 1 1999 **for those who met the criteria**. When stage 3 begins, all the participating members will agree the conversion rates at which their currencies will be exchanged for ECUs. The ECU will then be a currency in its own right and usable in shops and banks in all those countries that have moved to full monetary union.

The European System of Central Banks will have as its main objective to maintain price stability. It will also define and implement the Community's monetary policy; conduct foreign exchange operations; hold and manage official exchange reserves and promote the smooth operation of payment systems.

The European Central Bank will be consulted and be entitled to forward opinions on proposed Community and national acts within its field of competence while member states move towards monetary union. Once monetary union is established, the ECB may take over the functions of the EMI. It will have the exclusive right to authorise the issue of banknotes in the Community, both by the European or national central banks, but respecting, as far as possible, existing practices for their issuing and design. Member states will be able to issue coin subject to the ECB's approval. Only the European Council can introduce measures to harmonise denominations and the technical specifications of coins.

Both the European Central Bank and the national central banks must be independent, not taking instructions from anyone, whether EC institutions, governments or any other body.

NB The United Kingdom negotiated an opt-out for these procedures. If it chose to "opt in" to stage 3, it would need to notify the Council by December 31 1996 or by January 1 1998, if the Community takes the slower path.

Chapter 6

Subsidiarity
★ ★ ★ ★ ★ ★ ★ ★ ★ ★ ★ ★

The principle of subsidiarity is contained in Article 3B, which states that in the areas which do not fall under its executive jurisdiction, the Community will only take action when the objectives cannot be sufficiently achieved by the member states.

The Community is legally bound by the Treaty to adhere to this principle and no doubt it will be the subject of litigation before the Court of Justice. Quite clearly, some areas of policy can only be achieved by collective Community action. For example, removing the barriers to create an open market can only be achieved if each country accepts the rules and plays by them. This means the Community has to insist on certain standards for all countries which, for some people, has seemed both irritating and unnecessary.

It does not take a great deal of thought, however, to realise that a product should be safe if it is to be sold across borders. The failure to ensure common standards could swiftly lead to chaos and confusion not to mention genuine health and safety problems. For example, the failure to ensure safe pharmaceuticals, foodstuffs and building materials, could lead to serious loss of life. In the same way, everyone from pensioners to investment companies need to be certain that common and sufficiently high financial regulations apply throughout the Community if they are to avoid being swindled.

On the other hand, it is increasingly important to many people that the Community does not meddle in areas that can best be handled by national, or even local and regional government.

In other words: keep out of our "nooks and crannies" unless the issue is too large to be handled by the member state alone.

Chapter 7

Citizenship of the Union
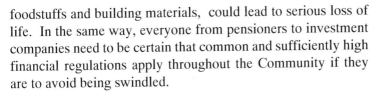

At the centre of the European Union is the concept that all citizens of member states* should also share in the rights and responsibilities that go with belonging to the European Union as a whole. If people are to move freely, it is important that they can also feel that they have certain rights that derive from their common citizenship of the Union.

The Treaty of Maastricht establishes this new idea by declaring that every person holding the nationality of a member state shall be a citizen of the Union and enjoy the rights and duties conferred upon citizens by the Treaty.

More precisely, these rights include:

★   the right to move freely within the Community, subject to the Community's laws (such as, in some cases, requiring

---

* These rights only apply to nationals of individual member states and not to third country nationals resident in the Community.

proof that a person will not require social assistance and has adequate health insurance);

★ the right to vote and stand as a candidate in local and European Parliament elections in whichever member state a citizen resides i.e. the right to vote in these elections will be based upon residency not nationality, though this will not apply to national general elections;

★ the right to diplomatic or consular representation by the diplomatic or consular authorities of any members state if you get into trouble in a third country (i.e. one that is not a member state of the EC);

★ the right to bring complaints about maladministration by Community institutions before an Ombudsman who will be appointed by the European Parliament and will be able to conduct independent investigations into allegations.

Additionally, the Treaty says that the Commission must report to the Council of Ministers every three years on the way that the provisions for citizenship have been applied, and that, following the usual EC procedures for adopting legislation, citizens rights may be increased in the future.

European citizenship does not in any way remove, reduce or conflict with the rights and responsibilities of national citizenship but rather adds a new dimension to the lives of those who belong to the Community's member states.

Chapter 8

Reforming the Institutions
★ ★ ★ ★ ★ ★ ★ ★ ★ ★ ★ ★

One of the objectives of the Maastricht Treaty is to deal with some of the more glaring deficiencies in the Community's democratic accountability. As can be seen by looking at the relationship between the Commission, the European Parliament and the Council of Ministers, the Community still suffers from what has been called a "democratic deficit". Power in the Community rests primarily in the hands of the Council of Ministers, whose members, while nominally responsible to their home parliaments, meet behind closed doors and can rarely be forcefully challenged by back-benchers who often lack the time and expertise to follow the intricacies of Community legislation.

> ★ **One major**
> ★ **objective is to**
> ★ **deal with some**
> ★ **of the glaring**
> ★ **deficiencies**
> ★ **of the**
> ★ **Community's**
> ★ **democratic**
> ★ **accountability**

A number of member states - most especially Germany - have argued, therefore, that more power should be given to the one directly elected institution which is uniquely fitted to question and examine Community legislation - the European Parliament. Not surprisingly, Members of the European Parliament have also long campaigned for greater powers and they have been supported by an increasing number of people in all member states who wish to see the Community become more open and accountable.

The European Parliament

The Maastricht Treaty, while a long way from resolving the issue of greater democratic accountability, nevertheless stipulates greater powers for the European Parliament.

In certain major sectors, including internal market legislation, consumer protection, health, education and general environmental programmes, the Parliament is to have new powers of co-decision with the Council of Ministers. These will enable the Parliament to reject a proposal by an overall majority of its members if agreement cannot be reached between the two institutions in a joint Conciliation Committee. This will work as follows:

The Commission will make a proposal to the European Parliament and the Council of Ministers. The Parliament will give its opinion and the Council of Ministers will then adopt a "common position", in other words agree as to what they wish to do, acting under the qualified majority procedures. The Council will then inform the Parliament of its position.

★
★ **Maastricht**
★ **strengthens**
★ **democratic**
★ **accountability**
★ **by giving**
★ **Parliament**
★ **new powers of**
★ **co-decision**
★

If the Parliament approves the Council's position, or takes no decision, the Council can adopt the proposal and it will become law. But, if the Parliament votes to reject the Council's position by an absolute majority - a majority of all elected MEPs - the Council can then call a meeting of a Conciliation Committee which will comprise equal numbers from the Council and the Parliament. If this fails, and the Parliament again rejects the proposal, it will fall. In other words, the Parliament will have a final veto.

The Parliament, if it can get an absolute majority, can also propose amendments. If it does so, the Council has a further three months to approve the amended text by qualified majority or it can refuse to approve the amendments, in which case the Conciliation Committee is convened again and given six weeks to work on the text. If it approves a joint text, and the European Parliament approves it by a simple majority of votes cast, and the Council approves it by a qualified majority, it will be adopted. If either institution rejects it, it will be lost.

If the Conciliation Committee fails to agree, however, the Council has a further six weeks to confirm its original position with, perhaps some of the Parliament's amendments. The Parliament then has a further six weeks on top of that to reject the text by an absolute majority of its members.

In other words, the European Parliament gets a veto on certain areas of legislation which include internal market legislation.

In addition, if the European Parliament agrees by an overall majority that new European legislation is necessary, it can request the Commission to submit proposals. It can also, at the request of a quarter of its members, set up a temporary Committee of Enquiry to investigate contravention or maladministration in the implementation of Community Law - a crucial new benefit for all European citizens who can petition their MEPs to investigate areas where they believe the Community's institutions to have acted wrongly.

The Parliament is to draw up proposals for a uniform election procedure for European Parliamentary Elections covering all the Member States which must be agreed unanimously by the Council of Ministers. It will also have to agree on the size of the European Parliament in the light of enlargement. For example, the German government has requested another 18 seats to take into account its new size after German unification. It will have to be enlarged even further if it is to cope with the entry of all those who have applied to join.

The Treaty also extends the term of office of the Commission from four years to five to coincide with European Parliamentary elections and gives the Parliament the right to veto the appointment of Commissioners. This is a significant step forward in strengthening the democratic accountability of the Commission.

Chapter 9

General Provisions
- applying to the European Community
★ ★ ★ ★ ★ ★ ★ ★ ★ ★ ★ ★ ★

Included in the Treaty are a number of general provisions relating to the first pillar of the European Union. These various ideas and amendments are of considerable importance but do not each need a separate chapter heading. They range from education and health through to transport, economic and social cohesion and the environment.

Because more contentious issues have tended to dominate the headlines about the Treaty, these less dramatic issues have been neglected but are of great importance to the development of the Community.

Culture, education, vocational training & youth

The philosophy underlying Community activity in these areas is encapsulated in the phrase: "The Community (is) to develop quality education by encouraging cooperation between member states, supporting and complementing the action; but underlines respect for responsibility of member states for the content of teaching and their cultural and linguistic diversity."

But, action will be aimed at developing the European dimension in education, particularly through language teaching, encouraging the mobility of teachers, students, trainees and instructors, and by improving vocational training in order to assist vocational integration and re-integration into the the labour market.

The role of the Community will be to generate new ideas and encourage cooperation between member states while respecting the enormous cultural and educational diversity in the Community. Its role is not to determine policy for the whole of the European Community.

Specifically, the Treaty proposes that the Community contributes to the promotion of member states' cultures and at the same time promotes European identity and the European cultural dimension. For example, the Community will encourage cooperation between member states in a number of areas including disseminating the culture of European peoples, conserving cultural heritage, non-commercial cultural exchanges, artistic and literary creation including the audio-visual sector, and fostering relations with third countries and international organisations.

Member states have retained their prerogative by providing that laws under these headings would have to have the unanimous support of the Council of Ministers.

Public health and consumer protection

The Community will continue to play a part in ensuring that consumers' interests and safety are protected in the single market and specific action will be taken to support and suppplement the policies of the member states. Community action will not be taken, however, to stop member states from maintaining or introducing more stringent measures.

In health matters, the Community will again play a role in co-ordinating and liaising between member states on health care programmes and will do what it can to contribute to raising standards of health care protection throughout the EC.

Trans-European networks & industry

Bearing in mind the need to increase economic activity in the single market, the Community will contribute to the development of trans-European networks in areas such as transport, telecommunications and energy infrastructures. It will also help to promote greater inter-connection and inter-operability between national networks and between the centre of the EC and those countries and regions on the periphery. Some funding will be provided to assist projects between member states.

For industry, the Community is to continue to favour conditions for competitiveness and structural changes to foster enterprise and to better exploit new and innovative developments.

Research & technological development

This section of the Treaty establishes that the overall programme of Community activities in this sphere should be agreed by unanimity but that individual programmes can be adopted by qualified majority voting.

★ **By providing**
★ **help to the**
★ **poorer regions**
★ **of the EC, the**
★ **Community aims**
★ **to increase**
★ **prosperity**
★ **and stable**
★ **government**

It also restates the need for the Community and member states to co-ordinate their Research & Development activities.

Economic and social cohesion

From the very start, the European Community has always believed that assistance should be provided to the poorer regions of the Community so that by promoting their economic growth and ability to trade, the whole Community would prosper. In other words, providing assistance to the poorer regions has a self-interested as well as an altruistic purpose. The more each region develops and is able to increase the sum total of Community trade - both internal and external - the more the Community as a whole will prosper. At the same time, increasing prosperity in the poorer areas will bolster stable and democratic government.

The name given to this process by the Community is "Economic and Social Cohesion". The necessary reallocation of resources is handled through the regional and structural funds.

It has been recognised by the member states that the single market and monetary union with its requirement that member states' economies must converge, would not be possible without the transfer of resources from the richer to the poorer regions of Europe.

Articles 130a to 130f reaffirm those principles. For example, Article 130a states:

> *"In order to promote its overall harmonious development, the Community shall develop and pursue its actions leading to the strengthening of its economic and social cohesion. In particular, the Community shall aim at reducing disparities between the levels of development of the various regions and the backwardness of the least-favoured regions, including rural areas."*

Environment

Protecting the environment has played an increasingly important part in Community legislation since the Single European Act. The Maastricht Treaty takes the process further by outlining the following objectives:

★ preserving, protecting and improving the quality of the environment;

★ protecting human health;

★ prudent and rational utilisation of natural resources;

★ promoting measures at international level to deal with regional or world-wide environmental problems.

Community policy on the environment will aim at a high level of protection taking into account the diversity of situations in the various regions of the Community. It will be based on the precautionary principle and on the principles that preventive action should be taken, that environmental damage should as a priority be rectified at source and that the polluter should pay.

The Treaty also insists that environmental protection requirements must be integrated into the definition and implementation of other Community policies.

In preparing its policy relating to the environment, the Community will take account of:

★ available scientific and technical data;

★ environmental conditions in the various regions of the Community;

★ the potential benefits and costs of action or lack of action;

★ the economic and social development of the Community as a whole and the balanced development of its regions.

However, further articles include some qualifications. Some issues including provisions relating to fiscal matters, town and country planning and land use and measures significantly affecting members states' choices between energy sources, will be subject to unanimous voting in the Council of Ministers. On the other hand, if the Council agrees unanimously, it can refer some of these matters to qualified majority voting. In other words, member states may choose, on some of these environmental issues, to give up their right of veto.

Although most environmental measures will be paid for by the member states, some the Community may finance directly.

Development cooperation

The Treaty reaffirms the Community's commitment to integrating the economies of the developing nations into the world economy and to the protection of democracy and human rights.

Committee of the Regions

It is becoming increasingly clear that Europe is not just about states, but also about regions and regional identity. Recognising this new trend, the Maastricht Treaty proposes a Committee of the Regions which must be consulted by the Council and the Commission in all cases where they consider it appropriate. Members of the Committee will be recommended by their national governments and appointed by the Council of Ministers. In all, the Committee wil have 189 members, 24 of whom will be from the United Kingdom. They will not be mandated by anyone but will have complete independence to make their own recommendations.

Additional provisions

There are finally a small number of additional provisions covering important areas which should be noted:

★ confirmation of the total free movement of capital between member states and member states and third countries (i.e. countries not within the Community);

   NB Those interested in the tax and other implications of the free movement of capital should look at articles 49 - 73h.

★ the application of common rules governing international transport and cabotage; (article 75)

★ the role of the European Parliament in determining which third country nationals should have visas for external border crossings;

★ the criteria for imposing visa requirements in the event of an emergency influx of nationals from third countries. (for further details see articles 92 - 100d).

Chapter 10

A Common Foreign and Security Policy - The Second Pillar of the Union
★ ★ ★ ★ ★ ★ ★ ★ ★ ★ ★ ★ ★

As has been explained earlier, the European Union that will be created by the Maastricht Treaty has a wider mandate than the European Community, which is just one of three pillars.

The second pillar will be Foreign and Security Policy Cooperation and it will operate far more, though not exclusively, through inter-governmental cooperation rather than through the institutions of the Community.

Many people have complained that European reaction to the most critical events in international relations during the past few years, for example the Gulf War and the Yugoslavian crisis, has been at best ragged and, at worst, chaotic. The responses of the different member states have seemed unco-ordinated and, occasionally, at odds with each other.

One answer is that European response has been inadequate precisely because the machinary did not exist to allow member states to co-ordinate their responses swiftly and effectively. The result has been that member states while recognising increasingly the need to discuss these matters with their partners, have not been able to exert the influence that their collective importance would merit.

If, as may tragically prove to be the case, the horrific Yugoslavian crisis is a foretaste of what may befall other parts of central and eastern Europe, there is a widely recognised need to increase substantially foreign and security policy cooperation.

The key objectives of the common foreign and security policy, as set out in the Treaty, are:

★ to safeguard the common values, fundamental interests and independence of the European Union;

★ to strengthen the security of the Union and its member states,

★ **The development and consolidation of democracy and the rule of law are key objectives of the Treaty**

★ to preserve peace and strengthen international security in accordance with the provisions of the United Nations Charter and the Helsinki Act (which created the Conference on Security and Cooperation in Europe (CSCE) - a forum for all the nations of Europe as well as the United Sates and Canada);

★ to promote international cooperation; and

★ to develop and consolidate democracy and the rule of law, and respect for human rights and fundamental freedoms.

The aim is to allow the European Union to "assert its identity on the international scene". In other words to play a part which is proportional to its size and economic strength.

Essentially, the governments of member states and the Commission will consult each other on matters of foreign and security policy and work together to implement the objectives as set out in the Treaty.

Where necessary, the Council of Ministers will take common positions on issues when they arise and they will decide whether or not there should be joint action. When a common position is taken, member states must ensure that their national policies conform to it.

The European Council (the meeting of the Community's leaders) will define the general policy guidelines. The Council of Ministers will normally take decisions unanimously but will define those matters where qualified majority voting can be used.

For those decisions which have defence implications, the European Union will ask for the help of the Western European Union to implement them.

The operational role of the WEU will be strengthened, with a planning cell, closer military cooperation, regular meetings of Chiefs of Defence Staff and more cooperation in the armaments field with the aim of creating a European armaments agency.

Although the European Commission will be associated with the decision making process and the European Parliament will be kept informed, Common Foreign and Security decisions will not use the same decision making processes as the European Community which are set out in Chapter 19. Nevertheless, the Commission may refer to the Council of Ministers questions on foreign and security policy, and the European Parliament will be consulted, will be able to put questions and recommendations to the Council and will hold an annual debate on the progress towards implementing common policies.

In an emergency, a meeting of the Council of Ministers can be called within 48 hours and the President of the Council (whichever country has the Presidency of the Community for that six months) will be responsible for ensuring that policy is carried out.

The Treaty also makes it quite clear that the new foreign and security policy procedures will not prejudice the specific defence and security policies of individual member states in NATO including the development of closer cooperation between two or more member states.

Summary

In brief, what these provisions will mean is the development of closer cooperation between member states acting through the Council of Ministers and leading to common positions on key issues. In the area of defence, the WEU will assist in the implementation of the decisions and keep Europe within the Atlantic Alliance .

Chapter 11

Justice and Home Affairs
- The Third Pillar of the Union
★ ★ ★ ★ ★ ★ ★ ★ ★ ★ ★ ★ ★

The third pillar of the European Union that is outlined in the Maastricht Treaty deals with the issues of justice, home affairs and immigration.

These are clearly matters of vital importance not just for the internal security of the European Community but also of relevance to those concerned with the protection of civil liberties and human rights.

They came out of a number of major concerns facing the Community including terrorism, the increase in drugs trafficking, and the increasing numbers of migrant workers, especially from the new democracies in eastern and central Europe looking for both work and, in some cases, refuge from civil unrest and war.

Although the Commission will be associated with the decision making procedures, justice and home affairs will remain an inter-governmental pillar of the Union Treaty. Indeed, they have always been dealt with on that basis since the Community's inception.

The provisions identify eight areas of common interest:

★ asylum policy;

★ crossing of the Community's external borders;

★ immigration policy;

★ combatting drug addiction;

★ judicial cooperation in civil and criminal matters;

★ customs cooperation;

★ police cooperation.

In these areas, joint positions and joint action can be taken by the Council, which can decide that certain measures may be adopted by a qualified majority. Only member states will have powers of initiating action in criminal matters, and not the Commission although the Commission will be fully associated with the work. The European Parliament will be informed and consulted and its views *"duly taken into consideration"*. The provisions make special reference to the European Convention on Human Rights and the Convention on the Status of Refugees and have *"regard to the protection afforded by member states to persons persecuted on political grounds"*

Immigration procedures will be dealt with under a "twin track" procedure. Under the Treaty of Rome, the Council will decide by unanimity on the basis of a Commission proposal which third countries require a visa to enter the European Community. But, from January 1 1996, this will change to qualified majority voting. In the case of a sudden crisis, emergency action can be taken for six months.

Issues such as asylum policy, which is aimed to be harmonised by the end of 1993, rules and controls on persons crossing EC external borders, and conditions of movement and residence for immigrants and illegal immigrants will be decided by inter-governmental agreement.

Finally, a Community-wide system for exchanging information between European police forces - EUROPOL - is to be set up.

Chapter 12

The Social Dimension - A separate protocol
★ ★ ★ ★ ★ ★ ★ ★ ★ ★ ★ ★

Because the United Kingdom was not prepared to sign the Treaty if it included a Social Chapter, a separate protocol implementing its provisions was signed by the other 11 member states.

Among the provisions of this protocol are:

★ supplementing the existing Community provisions in the social area including the objective of proper social protection, promotion of dialogue between management and labour, and development of human resources with a view to lasting high employment;

★ implementing measures to take account of diverse forms of national practices, in particular in the field of contractual relations and need to maintain competitiveness of the Community economy;

★ supporting and complementing member states activities in protecting workers' health and safety, working conditions, informing and consulting workers, equal opportunity and treatment and integration of people excluded from the labour market;

The protocol also reinforces Community rules on equal pay for men and women.

Additionally, the Commission would have the task of promoting dialogue between social partners (a reference to workforce and management). Further, the Council can act unanimously - for those member states who have signed the protocol - on social security and social protection, the protection of workers when their contracts are terminated, the conditions of employment for third country nationals and financial contributions for the promotion of employment.

Before submitting social policy proposals, however, the Commission should consult the "social partners" on the advisability of Community action.

Normally, the Commission consults the European Economic and Social Commitee, which is made up of appointees from both sides of industry and other interested parties from the member states.

Chapter 13

Budgetary Control
★ ★ ★ ★ ★ ★ ★ ★ ★ ★ ★ ★

The Maastricht Treaty tightens up control of the Community's finances by outlining a number of important measures including an insistence that when proposing new measures, the Commission must give assurances that these can be financed within the limits of the EC's financial resources. The Court of Auditors which monitors legally the Community's accounts becomes a full EC institution; the European Parliament will be able to ask the

Commission to give evidence regarding spending and financial control and expect it to act on the Parliament's decisions and observations; and governments will be required to deal with fraud affecting the Community's financial interests in the same way that they deal with national fraud.

PART THREE

Chapter 14

Europe - Past, Present & Future
★ ★ ★ ★ ★ ★ ★ ★ ★ ★ ★ ★ ★

The idea of a united Europe is not new. Remedies to a thousand years of fratricidal and bloody disputes between European nations have long been sought by both political thinkers and practical politicians. But it was only after the First and Second World Wars with their unparalled brutality and loss of life - amounting to the death of over 40 million people - that the first practical steps were taken towards building a united Europe.

In fact, until relatively modern times, Europe was widely perceived by those who lived there as a cultural entity with the relatively free movement of scholars, artists and traders. The Roman Empire, which covered much of what we now know as Western Europe, had brought to a largely tribal continent universal laws, a common language for the educated elite and a degree of economic interdependence. By the time of its demise Christianity, although divided between Roman Catholicism and Eastern Orthodoxy, was fast becoming the common religion of Europe.

When Charlemagne was crowned Emperor by the Pope on Christmas day 800 AD, his empire bore a remarkable resemblance to the territory now covered by the European Community. In the Middle Ages, Europe was known as "Christendom" and became the target for conquest by many who sought to unite it by a mixture of diplomacy and force of arms. Others tried the force of reason: a number of thinkers as varied as William Penn, Leibnitz, Montesquieu, Kant and, in more modern times, Lord

Lothian, Lord Beveridge, Barbara Wootton and Lionel Robbins advocated some form of a united Europe as a way to preserve peace for posterity.

It was not until less than fifty years ago, however, that serious and practical steps were taken to turn the vision into a practical reality.

Chapter 15

The Congress of Europe
★ ★ ★ ★ ★ ★ ★ ★ ★ ★ ★ ★ ★

In 1948, Winston Churchill chaired the Congress of Europe, which was held in The Hague. The Congress, concerned to foster reconciliation between former enemies, committed itself to working for the economic, political and cultural union of Europe.

The Congress led to *three* practical steps:

1. The establishment of the **Council of Europe**, whose Assembly is open to representatives from the parliaments of all democratic European states and which has 27 members at present. The Council is a forum for discussing all matters of common European importance: economic, political, cultural, environmental and social issues but it can only make recommendations to governments.

   Since 1989, its role has expanded to include some of the new democracies of central and eastern Europe and it has accepted as observers Russia and some other members of the Commonwealth of Independent States;

2. The drafting of a **European Convention on Human Rights**, backed by a Court of Human Rights. (Most European countries in the Council have incorporated the Convention

into their laws; UK has not, but recognises the Court as the final Court of Appeal), and

3. Set up the **European Movement** as a "people to people", voluntary organisation to bring about Economic, Monetary and Political Union in Europe.

The mood of the Congress of Europe was substantially *federalist*. Federalism is a "form of government of which the essential principle is a union of two or more states under one body for certain permanent common objects (Latin: **foedus**, a league)." However, embodied in Federalism is the principle of **subsidiarity** which holds that only such power as is necessary should be held by the centre; all other powers should be exercised at the lowest level compatible with efficiency.

★ **As the**
★ **forerunner of**
★ **the EC, the ECSC**
★ **bound together**
★ **France and**
★ **Germany, the**
★ **countries at the**
★ **centre of both**
★ **World Wars**

1951-52 The European Coal and Steel Community

In a revolutionary scheme to bind together those countries that had been at the centre of the conflict in both world wars - France and Germany, French Foreign Minister Robert Schuman and Jean Monnet proposed a common framework for the production and distribution of French and German coal and steel. In the Schuman Declaration of 1950, the key ideas underlying the building of modern Europe are outlined:

> *"Europe will not be made all at once, or according to a single plan. It will be built through concrete achievements which will first create a de facto solidarity. The coming together of the nations of Europe requires the elimination of the age-old opposition of France and Germany.....*
>
> *The pooling of coal and steel production should immediately provide for the setting up of common foundations for economic development as a first step in the federation of*

*Europe, and will change the destinies of those regions which
have long been devoted to the manufacture of munitions of
war, of which they have been the most constant victims."*

The European Coal and Steel Community was founded in 1952
and it was joined by France, Germany, Italy and the Benelux
countries (Belgium, The Netherlands and Luxembourg).

For the first time in their history, national governments delegated
part of their sovereignty, albeit in limited, clearly defined matters,
to a High Authority consisting of persons chosen by them but
acting independently, and collectively enjoying powers to take
decisions in the common interest of the Member States.

The United Kingdom, while invited to join, declined to do so.

Although the creation of a Defence Community and a Political
Community were put forward in the early 1950s, they met with
opposition from the French Parliament and were temporarily
dropped.

Chapter 16

The Treaty of Rome 1957
★ ★ ★ ★ ★ ★ ★ ★ ★ ★ ★ ★

Despite disappointment that the impetus towards European unity
was slowed down by the failure of the Defence and Political
Communities to bear fruit, the next step came soon.

On March 25 1957, the six members of the Coal and Steel
Community signed the Treaties of Rome which created the
European Economic Community (Common Market) and
Euratom.

The EEC's immediate objective was to attain freedom of
movement throughout the Community for goods, persons,

services and capital. In order to do so, it established a customs union by dismantling all quotas and tariff barriers to internal trade while establishing a common external tariff for goods imported from third party countries.

The Treaty also provided for common policies on:

★ agriculture. The Common Agricultural policy, which set up price support systems for farmers in order to boost their production and incomes;

★ transport & competition;

★ external trade;

★ the harmonisation of legislation.

It also set up the common institutions of the Community:

★ the Commission;

★ the Parliament;

★ the Council of ministers;

★ the Court.

These were practical steps towards Economic Union. The Treaty also envisaged, however, that the Community would in time move towards full Economic and Political Union.

Why did Britain not join?

At the time, successive British governments still believed that Britain had a unique role in the world at the point where three circles of influence: the Atlantic relationship, the Commonwealth and Europe met. She was prepared to join the much looser European Free Trade Association (EFTA) with the Scandinavian countries, Austria and Switzerland but felt she could stay outside the EEC.

This proved to be a major miscalculation. Very soon, it was noticeable that belonging to a Common Market had given a major boost to the economies of the six which grew much faster than the UK. Many countries sought associated status with the EEC and Britain began to realise that it had to negotiate for entry.

In the sixties, the United Kingdom twice negotiated entry into the Community but was vetoed both times by the French President General de Gaulle.

By 1973, however, the negotiations were successfully concluded and the United Kingdom, with Denmark and the Republic of Ireland signed the Treaty of Rome and became members of the European Economic Community, often called "the Common Market".

The Labour government, which had come to power in 1974, decided that so momentous a decision with constitutional implications should be put to a referendum of the British people and in 1975, after a major campaign with both sides being joined by members from all parties, those voting YES to staying in the Community won by 67.8% to 32.2% of the vote.

In 1981, Greece joined the EEC and in 1986, Spain and Portugal joined, making the Community of 12 as we now know it.

Problems

Getting a Community of 12 nations, with 9 languages, to work in harmony was a difficult enough problem but it was made much harder by the oil crisis of 1973, which had severe effects upon production, employment and inflation.

There were also problems with the Common Agricultural Policy, which, because of protectionist policies towards farmers and the green and technological revolutions, was leading to massive over-production: the wine lakes and grain, butter and beef mountains. These lasted until the Brussels summit of 1988, when British pressure forced their reduction using a system of stabilisers which brought the price down once a certain level of either production or market-price was reached.

The Cost of "non-Europe"

More serious, however, was the fact that the European Community was beginning to fall behind economically in comparison to its main trading rivals: the US and Japan. Most particularly in respect of high technology manufacture, Europe did not seem to be able to compete successfully with Japan and the newly emerging nations of the Pacific Rim - Hong Kong, South Korea, Taiwan, Singapore etc.

This failure to compete was showing itself particularly in the European unemployment figures of the 70s and early 80s which were dramatically worse than those of the US and Japan.

The Community related the reason for this failure to what became known as the "Cost of non-Europe", most clearly set out in the Cecchini Report. Acting on behalf of the Commission, Paolo Cecchini led a project composing a number of studies, including a survey of over 11,000 business people throughout Europe to find out what the remaining barriers to intra-EC trade were costing them.

The results were startling:

★ The cost of the physical barriers, i.e. waiting to go through customs and immigration and filling in forms etc., nominated by most business people as the most frustrating of all the barriers, was around **12 billion ECU** per year. (An ECU was then worth about 70p).

★ Discrimination against non-national tendering for public procurement contracts, accounting for over 15% of EC GDP, cost the Community over **40 billion ECU**. Most national and local governments discriminated in favour of home industries which stopped them buying the cheapest or most efficient goods or services.

★ The cost to industry of having different standards and specifications for different countries was almost impossible to quantify, yet probably was the largest cost of all. For example: a computer manufacturer in California can make one product available to all the other 49 states in the US and can, therefore, aim at a market of 240 million people with one product. In Europe, there was no such economy of scale even though the potential market is 350 million people.

★ Finally, Research & Development costs were much increased by scientists and researchers having to work in different national projects rather than as a Community.

Cecchini also calculated that if these barriers were removed and if there could be concerted macro-economic policy between the EC members, the Community could see an additional boost of 7% GDP and the creation of up to 5 million new jobs.

Chapter 17

The Single Europe Act
★ ★ ★ ★ ★ ★ ★ ★ ★ ★ ★ ★

In order to remove these barriers, and create a single European market, the EC first needed some new enabling legislation. In 1986, the Single European Act was passed as an amendment to the Treaty of Rome and was ratified by the Parliaments of all 12 Member States. It was called the **Single** European Act because it combined a number of issues within its terms of reference:

★ changes in the voting powers of the institutions;

★ removing the barriers;

★ environmental matters;

★ economic and social cohesion

★ the social dimension;

★ progress towards monetary union;

★ progress towards political co-operation on foreign affairs.

The Single European Market by 1993

The Act introduced the Parliament's right of amendment and the Council's qualified majority voting system for almost all legislation relating to the 1992 programme.

In order to remove the barriers to trade in the Community, a number of directives (laws) had to be passed. And, in order to set a tight timetable, the date for completion was set as the end of 1992.

The Directives

A British Commissioner, Lord Cockfield, was put in charge of drafting the directives necessary to removing the barriers and he outlined 300. They have since been reduced to 279 as some issues can be dealt with together.

The legislative burden would have been greater if the Community had not moved from a policy of detailed harmonisation of standards to one of minimal harmonisation together with *"mutual recognition"* i.e. if a product can legally be sold in one country it should be accepted by the other 11. BUT, areas that still needed harmonisation included:

★ health i.e. food, pharmaceuticals etc.;

★ safety i.e. toys, building materials etc.;

★ consumer protection i.e. financial services, banks, insurance policies, mortgages etc.;

★ academic, professional and vocational qualifications;

★ opening public procurement to Community-wide tender;

★ environmental standards;

★ VAT & excise duties;

★ frontier controls.

The Commission broke the directives into three groups:

★ **physical** i.e. customs & immigration (still subject to unanimity in the Council);

★ **technical** i.e. mutual standards & specifications (to be decided by Committees (Comite de Normalisation Europeen: CEN & CENELEC);

★ **fiscal** i.e. VAT (also subject to unanimity).

Progress on these groups has been very successful and at the time of publication (October 1992) over 90% of the directives have been agreed.

It is worth pointing out that the source of many of the irritations most frequently brought up by people in the Community derive not from the Maastricht Treaty but from the problems thrown up by the creation of a single market.

For example: the feeling that the Commission is interfering in a wide variety of areas that should not be its concern, such as French cheeses, British sausages, the content of jam etc., have come about because of the need to ensure that the goods people buy contain what the consumer think they contain and are safe from contamination or health dangers. The most obvious cases in point are toys and pharmaceuticals. If these goods are to circulate freely in the Community, then it is clearly vital that they do not present dangers to the consumer.

The same principle applied to a whole variety of products and services is what has caused much popular concern. To some extent, the problem will be lessened by the rigorous application of the principle of subsidiarity; nevertheless, consumers wishing to receive maximum protection may feel that the Commission's involvement in such areas is of continued importance.

Chapter 18

Enlargement of the Community
★ ★ ★ ★ ★ ★ ★ ★ ★ ★ ★ ★ ★

★ **Countries**
★ **wishing to join**
★ **must be**
★ **democracies,**
★ **free market**
★ **economies and**
★ **conform to**
★ **other rigorous**
★ **standards**

Europe is much larger than just 12 countries. The Community has committed itself to the principle of enlargement but those countries wishing to join must be democracies, able to conform to the standards of the European Convention on Human Rights, must be free market economies and able to meet the increasingly rigorous economic and environmental standards set by the EC. At the beginning of 1993, the agreement creating a European Economic Area, bringing together the EC and the 7 European Free Trade Area countries (Austria, Norway, Sweden, Finland, Switzerland, Iceland and Lichtenstein) into one single market will be a major step towards an enlarged Community.

Applications for full membership of the European Community have been received from Austria, Sweden, Finland and Switzerland, Cyprus, Turkey and Malta.

It is extremely likely that Czech and Slovak Republics, Hungary and Poland will wish to join as soon as they are able. Then the European Community will have to look at its relationship with the remaining eastern European countries including states previously in the former Soviet Union and now grouped together as the Commonwealth of Independent States.

Chapter 19

The Institutions of the European Community.

1. The Commission.
17 Commissioners appointed by the governments of the member states for fixed terms to *work for Europe* head a team of 13,000 European Civil Servants (Eurocrats). Two Commissioners are appointed from the larger countries and one each from the smaller countries. Their job is:

★ to initiate legislation to fulfill the aims and objectives of the treaties;

★ once, the legislation has been approved by the Parliament and the Council of Ministers, to carry it out. The current President of the Commission is Jacques Delors, a Frenchman, who will remain President until 1994;

★ to ensure the application of the treaties and Community legislation.

2. The Parliament.

The Parliament is directly elected by the people of Europe once every five years. Its 518 members, MEPs, sit in party groups i.e. Socialists, including the British Labour Party, the European Peoples Party, which includes Christian Democrats and the British Conservatives, the European Liberal Group, the Greens, Communists, the Far Right etc.

The Parliament has the right to pass or withold the budget, to sack the Commission and now, since the Single European Act, to amend legislation which, if supported by the Commission, can only be rejected by the Council of Ministers if the vote is unanimous.

The Parliament meets in Strasbourg but has offices in both Luxembourg and Brussels, a cumbersome procedure that is likely to have to change soon.

Its powers have been increased in the Maastricht Treaty.

3. The Council of Ministers.

This is not one Council but several: Environment Ministers, Trade, Education, Foreign, Health Ministers etc., each dealing with issues relevant to their Departments. Twice a year, at European Council meetings, the Heads of State meet to make overall decisions for the Community. The Council of ministers is backed up by permanent staff based in Brussels and by home civil servants travelling with them.

Until the Single European Act, the Council had to make unanimous decisions. Now they vote on most legislation by qualified majority. This system gives the UK, France, West Germany and Italy ten votes each, Spain eight votes, Belgium, Holland, Greece and Portugal five votes, Denmark and Ireland three votes and Luxembourg two votes. They have to reach a total of 54 out of 76 to pass legislation.

The Council shares executive power with the Commission and legislative power with the European Parliament.

4. The European Court of Justice.
This is the Court that interprets Community legislation and resolves disputes. It is based in Luxembourg and should not be confused with the Court of Human Rights sitting in Strasbourg. Its responsibility to define subsidiarity develops its role as the Supreme Court of Europe.

PART FOUR

Chapter 20

10 Myths About the Maastricht Treaty
★ ★ ★ ★ ★ ★ ★ ★ ★ ★ ★ ★

Myth 1. *Voting against Maastricht will stop all those aspects of European interference we most dislike.*

There is a widespread illusion that voting against Maastricht will - at a stroke - prevent the Commission from delving into the "nooks and crannies" of every day life. But it is not the Maastricht Treaty that has been responsible for the threat posed to the prawn-favoured crisp, the British sausage and all those other integral parts of British culture that are the stuff of the tabloid headlines. The harmonisation or mutual recognition of products that has been the source of these stories - themselves frequently legendary - derives from the underlying principles of a single European market as envisaged in the Treaty of Rome and developed in the Single European Act. If anything, the Maastricht Treaty begins to provide some redress over bureaucratic intrusions by introducing new rights of European citizenship including a European ombudsman and new ways to petition the European Parliament.

★
★ **The Maastricht**
★ **Treaty provides**
★ **some redress**
★ **over**
★ **bureaucratic**
★ **intrusions by**
★ **introducing new**
★ **rights**
★

Myth 2. *The Commission is forever seeking to meddle in the affairs of member states which should not concern it.*

Of all the misapprehensions about Community policy, this is possibly the most potent. It symbolises the frustration of the citizen confronted by a seemingly meddlesome and unaccountable bureaucracy. It is also unfair. At least 80% of the directives contained in the 1992 proposals are concerned with consumer protection in an open market and most were requested by one or more member state. Commission interference in defining and labelling foodstuffs may encourage cartoonists and leader writers to vent their spleen but it does not take much to imagine the headlines if a child was poisoned by an undeclared substance in a food or pharmaceutical product, or injured by a non-regulated toy. Or indeed, were a pension fund to go bust because European pension and insurance regulations were not applicable to some member states.

Myth 3. *The Commission has the power to decide.*

Another version of this myth is "Delors has succeeded, where Napoleon and Hitler failed in subjecting Europe to his will." It is a convenient myth for government ministers whose unpopular decisions in Council can be off loaded onto the Commission. In fact, it is not just the Commission's task, but its duty to propose legislation necessary to realise European integration as set out in the relevant treaties. The Parliament has limited powers of amendment but, in the final analysis, the Council decides.

Myth 4. *The Commission is unapproachable and unaccountable.*

Neither accusation is strictly true. Compared to the higher echelons of the British civil service, the Commission is extraordinarily approachable right up to the level of the Commissioners' private offices. At the very least, Commissioners' faces are seen regularly in public which is more than can be said for the average British Permanent Secretary. The lack of accountability is nearer the mark, though, in reality, a Commission out of control could and would be reined in by the Council. The only way to make it really accountable, however, is to strengthen the powers of the European Parliament and Maastricht is a step in that direction.

Myth 5. *Maastricht will diminish the powers of the Westminster Parliament and so take power away from the British people.*

The House of Commons has never been able to scrutinise successfully European legislation in time to alter it. If anything, it is the House of Lords which has produced the most thorough analyses of European legislation. But, in reality, there is only one body that has both the democratic legitimacy and the ability to demand accountability - the European Parliament.

Myth 6. *Federalism cannot work. Look at the collapse of the Soviet Union and Yugoslavia.*

This is just a semantic argument. In neither example was there a real federation. The word was used to cover up a totalitarian empire in the former case and an externally imposed solution maintained by repressive force in the latter. Federations require democratic legitimacy to survive. As it stands, the European Community is a balance between federal institutions - the Commission, the Court and the Parliament, and a con-federal institution, the Council of Ministers which ultimately holds power in the name of the member states. The question European citizens should ask is: "Which of these institutions is ultimately more able to represent the wishes of the people of Europe?"

Myth 7. *The EC threatens the survival of the British Monarchy*

There are six constitutional monarchies in the EC - Belgium, Denmark, Holland, Luxembourg, Spain and the UK. They all have royal families who, to different degrees, symbolise the history and aspirations of their peoples and command their loyalty. No-one can say whether or not this will ever change, but it will not be because of the European Community. In no sense does the EC threaten the Queen's place as Head of the United Kingom and the Commonwealth. For example, bank notes issued in a common currency can continue to carry the Queen's portrait in the UK and those of the other monarchs in their respective countries.

Myth 8. *Subsidiarity is the struggle for power between Brussels and the member states.*

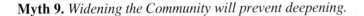

It has come to seem like that, but subsidiarity means more than just a tussle between national and supra-national governments. Theoretically, it also allows for the devolution of power to lower levels of government compatible with efficiency - for example, regional and local government. Indeed, much of the German anxiety about Maastricht is that it still leaves to much power with the members states rather than the regions of the Community.

Myth 9. *Widening the Community will prevent deepening.*

Quite the opposite is true. Nothing will make deepening more urgent than the institutional problems that will be caused by enlargement. Quite rightly, the British government has made enlargement a top priority of its Presidency. But it will soon be seen that 18 or more members states will throw existing inadequacies into sharp relief. Already there are too many Commissioners for efficient management; a presidency every nine years or more will hardly be an enormous incentive; the use of the veto in the Council will become an impossible luxury. Somewhere along the line, it will become obvious that only the federal institutions will be able to tackle the tasks successfully.

Myth 10. *Just looking at the Gulf and Yugoslavia shows the failure of a European Common Foreign and Defence Policy.*

What these two conflicts show is the failure of Europe to develop in time a common foreign and defence policy able to react swiftly and effectively. Unless the necessary mechanisms are developed as a priority, Europe will face untold dangers in the not too distant future. Yugoslavia is providing a taster of far worse potential conflicts in the CIS and other trouble spots on our doorstep. Time is fast running out when the European Community can afford the luxury of internal disputes.

There are, of course, numerous other myths that will continue to be widely believed about the Community. Perhaps the worst of all is that the point of European unity is free trade and material prosperity. For those who have been sold the idea of Europe on that limited basis, success must seem uninspiring and failure dispiriting. But for those who see it as an answer to millennia of bloodshed, it is a miracle.

MEMBERSHIP APPLICATION FORM

The European Movement campaigns for:

★ full European monetary, economic and political union

★ an open, accountable and democratic Community

★ early entry for all democratic, free market, European nations

★ the ratification of the Maastricht Treaty

I would like more information   Yes/No*

I wish to join   Yes/No*

Surname: (Mr/Mrs/Miss/Ms*) ....

First name(s):   ....

Address: ....

....

....

.... Postcode ....

Telephone: (STD Code) ....

Annual subscription £15. Couples £20. Students/OAP's £5

Access/VISA* No: ....

Expiry Date: ....

I enclose a cheque made out to
"The European Movement" for £: ....

Date: ....

Signed: ....

(* Delete as appropriate)

Please return to:
EUROPEAN MOVEMENT
Europe House, 158 Buckingham Palace Road, London, SW1W 9TR
Tel: 071-824 8388, Fax: 071-824 8124